WAY OF THE CROSS
WITH THE CHURCH IN NEED

Illustrated by James Grint

Aid to the Church in Need

D1533952

Published by Aid to the Church in Need
1 Times Square
Sutton
Surrey SM1 1LF
Great Britain
Registered Charity no. 265582

Imprimatur

Cover design & illustrations © James Grint

Printed by Caldra House
23 Coleridge Street
Hove, Sussex BN3 5AB
Great Britain

ISBN 0951 1805

FOREWORD

The narrative for this Way of the Cross is made up largely of quotations from the Gospels; the narrative of the events not reported in the Gospels is taken from the Via Crucis meditations for the Lenten retreat of Pope Paul VI in 1976, which was preached by the then Archbishop Wojtyla of Cracow. The Meditations for each Station are taken from the words and writings of the Holy Father; the intentions and prayers are for the Church in need in so many parts of the world ~ but also for ourselves, that we too may live up to the sublime vocation to which all Christians are called as sons and daughters of God. May we make our own the invitation of our Holy Father, Pope John Paul II:

The whole church, Pastors and lay faithful alike, must feel more strongly the Church's responsibility to obey the command of Christ: "Go into the all the world, and preach the Gospel to the whole of creation", and take up anew the missionary endeavour. A great venture, both challenging and wonderful, is entrusted to the Church: that of re-evangelisation... you, the lay faithful, ought to regard yourselves as an active and responsible part of this venture.

*Apostolic Exhortation **Christifideles laici**, 30th December 1988*

INTRODUCTION

Dear friend:

Abandoned and alone on a cross between heaven and earth, Jesus has ransomed us all. But it is only when we love him and when we are united to him that we possess the ransom for our sins and the key to heaven. Our union with him must be more precious to us than all the treasures that the earth can offer us.

But no-one can be united to him without taking part in his Passion and his Cross. That is why the Church is nowhere more flourishing than where she suffers persecution, where she is in need. And she is nowhere in greater danger than where she flees the solitude of Christ crucified.

Our Work gives you the possibility of taking part in the sufferings of Jesus. Across every frontier, we take something that belongs to you ~ a part of your heart, a handful of consolation, a cloth to dry their tears ~ to those countries where the Master is again making his Way of the Cross, where he hangs dying on the Calvaries of the twentieth century. Through us, you are able to lighten his Way of the Cross like Veronica or Simon of Cyrene, and stand at the foot of his Cross like Mary or John.

Do not turn away from this possibility. For nothing is more serious than to turn away heedlessly from Jesus who is suffering in his Church. And nothing is more precious than to console our abandoned Jesus, present in his persecuted brethren.

Do not think that it is a question of money: it is a question of love. Your financial sacrifice is worth nothing if it is made with ulterior motives, if your heart does not bleed for the pain of those who must bleed with the Lamb. It is only in sharing truly in the sufferings of your brothers in distress, in whom you recognise our Lord, that you can be united to the abandoned Jesus.

The consequences of this are beyond counting: for in him you possess God, in whom you find not only heaven with the Blessed Trinity, but also the earth with the whole of humanity. In him you possess all things, for all that is his becomes yours too.

So cling to the image of the Man of Sorrows who is crucified in millions of Christians. Do not let yourself be taken up by the little worries of each day to the point of forgetting the day that you must accept your last cross. Fight against your human respect, against cowardice and fear of suffering, against your passions and your sins.

Practise accepting the little crosses that God sends you. Deny yourself something ~ a real privation, of something which will console others ~ in order to lighten the Cross under which God's chosen are bowed down. And beg God to give those who bear the Cross alone the strength to share in the lot of the abandoned Jesus. Pray for the Church in need, for yourself, and also for your

Werenfried van Straaten, O.Praem.
Founder of Aid to the Church in Need

♦ I ♦

JESUS IS CONDEMNED TO DEATH

As Jesus came out, wearing the crown of thorns and the scarlet cloak, Pilate said to them, "See, here is the man." When the chief priests and their officers saw him, they cried out: "Crucify him, crucify him!" Pilate said to them, "Shall I crucify your king?" "We have no king," the chief priests answered, "except Caesar." At that, he gave Jesus up into their hands to be crucified. (Jn 19:5-6, 15-16)

Meditation

"Holding the high priesthood as he did in that year, Caiphas was able to prophesy that Jesus was to die for the sake of the nation; and not only for that nation's sake, but so as to bring together into one all God's children scattered far and wide" (Jn 11:51-52).

John does not hesitate to attribute to these words of Caiphas a prophetic meaning, as a revelation of the divine plan. It was indeed part of this plan that Christ, through his redemptive sacrifice which reached its summit with the death on the Cross, should become the source of a new unity of mankind, who are called in him ~ Christ ~ to rediscover their dignity as the adopted sons of God. In this sacrifice on the Cross can be found the origin of the Church as the community of salvation.

General Audience, 6th October 1991

Let us pray

We pray for those unjustly accused and unjustly condemned because of their faith, that they may feel the joy of knowing that they are suffering for righteousness' sake, in union with you.

Lord, hear us.

We pray that we may not rashly judge those around us, but be ready always to understand, to excuse, and to forgive.

Lord, hear us.

Lord Jesus Christ, first-born of many brethren, you are alone and mistreated all over the world today. May we be more attentive to the sufferings of others, and so grow more like you, who live and reign for ever and ever.

Amen.

JESUS TAKES UP HIS CROSS

They, once he was in their hands, led him away. So Jesus went out, carrying his own cross, to the place named after a skull; its Hebrew name is *Golgotha*. (Jn 19:16-17)

He said to all alike: "If any man has a mind to come my way, let him renounce self, and take up his cross daily, and follow me. He who tries to save his life will lose it; it is the man who loses his life for my sake that will save it." (Lk 9:23-4)

Meditation

In the midst of this vigil stands the cross.
You have borne this cross to this place and
you have erected it in the midst of our
gathering. On that cross, the divine 'I am' of
the new and eternal Covenant is made
manifest "to the very end" (Jn 13:1).

"God so loved the world that he gave up his
only-begotten Son, so that those who
believe in him may not perish, but have
eternal life" (Jn 3:16). The Cross, sign of
that unfathomable love; the sign that reveals
that "God is love" (Jn 4:8).

Meeting with youth
Czestochowa, 14th August 1991

Let us pray

We pray for our Christian brothers and sisters who live, even now, under the yoke of persecution, and for those who have lived and died in prisons and labour camps.

Lord, hear us.

We pray that each of us may be always ready to respond to your invitation to deny ourselves in the little things of each day.

Lord, hear us.

Lord Jesus, you said: "Come to me, you who are heavy laden, and I will give you rest." Take pity on your Church, threatened from within and without, delivered up before the world; support her with the strength of your arm, you who live and reign for ever and ever.

Amen.

◆ III ◆

JESUS FALLS
FOR THE FIRST TIME

Jesus falls under the weight of the cross. He falls to the ground. He does not resort to his supernatural power, nor does he resort to the power of angels. "Do you think that I cannot pray to my Father, who would at once send me more than twelve legions of angels?" (Mt 26:53). He does not ask for that. Having accepted the cup from his Father's hands (Mk 14:36), he is resolved to drink it to the end. (*Via Crucis*)

Meditation

No being in the world is exempt from weakness, whether physical, emotional or spiritual. Each of us must face up to our handicaps humbly. In the providence of God, this does not mean a lesser aptitude for holiness or for serving the world: on the contrary, we can do all things in him who strengthens us, Christ Jesus.

Every time we overcome the temptation to discouragement, every time we give proof of a joyful, generous and patient heart, we give witness to that Kingdom which is still to come in all its fullness, the Kingdom where we will be freed from every infirmity.

Meeting with the handicapped
Strasbourg 1988

Let us pray

We pray for all those who persecute our brothers and sisters in the faith and for those who collaborate with unjust authorities, that they may receive the grace of conversion and become your friends.

Lord, hear us.

We pray that we may recognise the times when we go astray, and may not be ashamed to turn back to you with true contrition.

Lord, hear us.

Lord Jesus, we ask you to give to our persecuted brethren the grace to accept the Cross which they have not chosen, and to follow in your path to the Father, who lives and reigns with you and the Holy Spirit for ever and ever.

Amen.

◆IV◆

JESUS MEETS HIS MOTHER

Simeon said to Mary: "Behold, this child is destined to bring about the fall of many and the rise of many in Israel, to be a sign which men will refuse to acknowledge: and so the thoughts of many hearts shall be made manifest. As for your own soul, it shall have a sword to pierce it." (Lk 2:34-5)

Mary meets her Son along the way of the Cross. His Cross becomes her Cross, his humiliation is her humiliation, the public scorn is on her shoulders. "A sword will pierce your soul": the words spoken when Jesus was forty days old are now coming true. (*Via Crucis*)

Meditation

Side by side with her Son, and faithfully persevering in union with her Son, she "advanced in her pilgrimage of faith", as the Council emphasises. This happened not without a divine plan: by suffering deeply with her only-begotten Son and joining herself with her maternal spirit to his sacrifice, lovingly consenting to the immolation of the victim to whom she had given birth, in this way Mary "faithfully preserved her union with her Son, even to the Cross."

How great, how heroic then is the obedience of faith shown by Mary in the face of God's "unsearchable judgments"! How completely she abandons herself to God without reserve, offering the full assent of the intellect and the will to him whose "ways are inscrutable" (Rom 11:33)!

Encyclical Letter Redemptoris Mater,
25th March 1987

Let us pray

We pray for children unjustly taken from their Christian parents, and for all children suffering from hardship, maltreatment, and neglect.

Lord, hear us.

We pray for the millions of starving people in the world, and for the victims of natural disasters: droughts and floods, hurricanes and earthquakes.

Lord, hear us.

Blessed Virgin, bend in sympathy over the children who are dying of hunger and cold. Take into your arms those who die in misery, O Virgin of Tenderness, and bring them into that Kingdom where every tear will be wiped away, the Kingdom where your Son lives and reigns for ever and ever.

Amen.

·**V**·

SIMON OF CYRENE HELPS JESUS TO CARRY THE CROSS

As for his cross, they forced a passer-by who was coming in from the country to carry it, one Simon of Cyrene, the father of Alexander and Rufus. (Mk 15:21)

Simon of Cyrene, called upon to carry the Cross, doubtless had no wish to do so: he was forced to. He made his way alongside Christ, bearing the weight himself. When the condemned man's shoulders became too weak, he lent him his own. He moved along very close to Jesus, closer than Mary, closer than John. (*Via Crucis*)

Meditation

"Even as I write, I am glad of my sufferings on your behalf, as, in this mortal frame of mine, I help to pay off the debt which the afflictions of Christ still leave to be paid, for the sake of his body, the Church" (Col 1:24). The truth of our faith does not exclude, but rather demands, the participation of man, of all men, in the sacrifice of Christ, in collaboration with the Redeemer. The Apostle Paul says so explicitly.

These statements do not come only from Paul's personal experience and understanding; they express the truth about man, ransomed, without any doubt, by the price of Christ's Cross, and yet at the same time called to "complete in his own flesh what is lacking" in Christ's sufferings for the Redemption of the world.

General Audience, 26th October 1988

Let us pray

We pray for the men of good will who, following the example of Simon of Cyrene, take up a part of your Cross in order to relieve the sufferings of your Church.

Lord, hear us.

We pray for the misery on our own door-steps: may God open the hears of Christians and move them to give their riches, their time, and their strength in the service of the poorest.

Lord, hear us.

Lord, just as Simon came to your aid, we wish to relieve the sufferings of your Church in need. Awaken in our hearts the wish to come to the aid of the pastors of your Church who live in the greatest of poverty: you who live and reign for ever and ever.

Amen.

·VI·

VERONICA WIPES
THE FACE OF JESUS

Tradition has bequeathed us Veronica ~ a counterpart to the man from Cyrene. Although, being a woman, she could not physically carry the Cross or be called upon to do so, there is no doubt that she really did carry it in the only way open to her at the time, in obedience to the dictates of her heart: she wiped his face. Tradition has it that an imprint of Christ's features remained on the handkerchief she used. (*Via Crucis*)

Meditation

As Veronica ministered to Christ on his way to Calvary, so Christians have accepted to care for those in pain and sorrow as privileged opportunities to minister to Christ himself. Remember it is Christ to whom you minister in the sufferings of your brothers and sisters; the wisdom of Christ and the power of Christ are to be seen in the weakness of those who share his sufferings.

Let us keep the sick and the handicapped at the centre of our lives. Let us treasure them and recognise with gratitude the debt we owe them. We begin by imagining that we are giving to them; we end by realising that they have enriched us.

Meeting with the sick
Southwark Cathedral, 28th May 1982

Let us pray

We pray for those disfigured by torture, maltreatment, false imprisonment, and every sort of oppression, so that their rights, and God's, may be clearly recognised.

Lord, hear us.

We pray for the oppressed and prisoners who await our help: may they be met with friendly faces.

Lord, hear us.

Lord Jesus, give us the strength to repeat Veronica's gesture and wipe away the tears of our brethren on your face, by sharing in their sufferings. Let them know the power of your Resurrection: you who live and reign for ever and ever.

Amen.

◆VII◆

JESUS FALLS A SECOND TIME

"I am a worm, not a man, scorned by all, the laughing-stock of the mob" (Ps 22:6): the words of the Psalmist come true in these steep, narrow little streets of Jerusalem in the last hours before the Passover, with the streets teeming with people.

The words of the Psalmist are coming true, even though nobody gives this a thought. Certainly it passes unnoticed by those who are displaying their scorn, people for whom this Jesus of Nazareth ~ now falling for the second time ~ has become a laughing-stock.

(*Via Crucis*)

Meditation

Faith in sharing in the suffering of Christ brings with it the interior certainty that the suffering person "completes what is lacking in Christ's afflictions"; the certainty that in the spiritual dimension of the work of Redemption he is serving, like Christ, the salvation of his brothers and sisters. It is precisely suffering, permeated by the spirit of Christ's sacrifice, that is the irreplaceable mediator of the good things that are indispensable for the world's salvation....

And so the Church sees in all Christ's suffering brothers and sisters a multiple subject of his supernatural power. How often is it precisely to them that the pastors of the Church appeal, and precisely from them that they seek help and support!

Apostolic Letter Salvifici Doloris,
11th February 1984

Let us pray

We pray for the leaders of churches which have suffered long persecution, that the example of Jesus may give them strength to live in the light of the truth.

Lord, hear us.

We pray for the young who have had the courage to reject atheism and materialism and who are thirsting for justice and truth, that they may find you who are the Way, the Truth, and the Life.

Lord, hear us.

Lord, you call us to follow you freely on the way of the Cross. Grant that your disciples may respond to that call, deny themselves, take up the Cross, and confess that you are the Saviour of mankind through your humbling of yourself and being raised to the right hand of the Father, where you live and reign for ever and ever.

Amen.

◆VIII◆

JESUS CONSOLES THE WOMEN OF JERUSALEM

Jesus was followed by a great crowd of the people, and also of women, who beat their breasts and mourned over him; but he turned to them and said:

"It is not for me that you should weep, daughters of Jerusalem; you should weep for yourselves and for your children... If it goes so hard with the tree that is still green, what will become of the tree that is already dried up?" (Lk 23:27-8, 31)

Meditation

Christ himself called, and still calls, his disciples to that participation. He speaks often, too, of the persecutions that await his disciples.

These texts of the New Testament, and others, have founded ~ and rightly so ~ the theological, spiritual and ascetic tradition which, since the earliest times, has upheld the necessity and shown the way of following Christ in his Passion, not just in imitation of his virtues but also in order to co-operate in the universal Redemption through participating in his sacrifice.

New Year Message, 1st January 1989

Let us pray

We pray for our brethren who are refugees from the countries of the Third World, for exiles and migrant workers, that they may find help and comfort from us.

Lord, hear us.

We pray for the formation of seminarians throughout the world, that they may persevere in their priestly vocations and confirm their brothers in the faith.

Lord, hear us.

Almighty and eternal God, you gather together what is scattered and unite what you have gathered. Look with love upon the flock of your Son: may the bond of charity and the fullness of the faith unite all who have been consecrated by the one baptism. We ask this through Christ our Lord.

Amen.

◆IX◆

JESUS FALLS
FOR THE THIRD TIME

"He became humbler still, making himself obedient even to death, death on the Cross" (Phil 2:8). We see Jesus falling for the third time under the Cross, falling, lying in the dusty road under the Cross, at the feet of a hostile crowd that spares him no insult or humiliation. (*Via Crucis*)

Meditation

To have a 'Paschal sense' to life also means
to understand the depths of the reality and
the value of the Redemption carried out by
the Passion and the death of Jesus on the
Cross, an *atoning sacrifice* which makes
us realise the gravity of sin ~ rebellion
against God and refusal of his love ~ as well
as the marvellous work of the Redemption
carried out by Christ who, making atone-
ment for humanity, has given back to us
grace, that is, the participation in the
Trinitarian life of God himself and the
pledge of eternal happiness.

General Audience, 7th May 1989

Let us pray

We pray for those who fall many times under the weight of the Cross, that you may save them from despair.

Lord, hear us.

We pray for bishops, priests, religious and laity who are tempted to deny their faith under persecution and hardship, that you may give them the grace to remain faithful.

Lord, hear us.

Father, give the light of hope to those who will know today both suffering and tears. We ask this through your Son Jesus Christ, our Lord.

Amen.

◆X◆

JESUS IS STRIPPED
OF HIS GARMENTS

The soldiers took up his garments, which they divided into four shares, one share for each soldier. They took up his cloak, too, which was without seam, woven from the top throughout; so they said to one another, "Better not to tear it; let us cast lots to decide whose it shall be." This was in fulfilment of the passage in Scripture which says, "They divide my spoils among them, cast lots for my clothing." So it was, then, that the soldiers occupied themselves. (Jn 19:23-4)

Meditation

In offering himself "as a ransom for many", Christ put completely into effect his solidarity with all men, with all sinners. But this solidarity was in no way an effect of sin on him: on the contrary, it was a gratuitous act of the purest love.

His solidarity with man in death consists, then, in the fact that not only did he die as men die ~ as all men die ~ but he died for all men. Thus his *substitution* signifies the *super-abundance* of love.

New Year Message, 1st January 1989

Let us pray

We pray for those suffering from poverty and nakedness, that their trust in you, their provident Father, may be rewarded through the efforts of Christians everywhere.

Lord, hear us.

We pray for all religious, that they may find in their poverty, freely embraced for the sake of the Kingdom of heaven, a spur to greater faithfulness and closer union with you.

Lord, hear us.

Lord, we are united indissolubly in love with those who, through love and faithfulness to Christ, must carry the Cross, stripped of everything. Strengthen our faith, so that our prayer may accompany our brethren at all times: you who live and reign for ever and ever.

Amen.

·XI·

JESUS IS NAILED TO THE CROSS

They offered him a draught of wine, mixed with gall, which he tasted, but would not drink; and then they crucified him. Jesus meanwhile was saying, "Father, forgive them: they do not know what it is they are doing." (Mt 27:34-5; Lk 23:34)

"They have pierced my hands and my feet, I can count all my bones" (Ps 22:16-17). How prophetic those words turned out to be! And yet we know that the whole of this body, hands, feet, and every bone, is a priceless ransom. "I, when I am lifted up from the earth, will draw all men to myself" (Jn 12:32): therein lies the full reality of the crucifixion. (*Via Crucis*)

Meditation

To a great extent, our Catholic unity depends on mutual charity. Let us remember that the unity of the Church originated on the Cross of Christ, which broke down the barriers of sin and division and reconciled us with God and one another. Jesus foretold this unifying act when he said: "... and I, if I be lifted up from the earth, will draw all men to myself" (Jn 12:32).

If we continue to imitate the love of Jesus, our Saviour, on the Cross, and if we persevere in love for one another, then we shall preserve the bonds of unity in the Church and witness the fulfilment of Jesus' prayer: "Father... that they may be one" (Jn 17:11).

Meeting with Catholic Bishops
Philadelphia, 4th October 1979

Let us pray

We pray for all the people of good will who work for a more just and fraternal world, that they may recognise you as their Father.

Lord, hear us.

We pray for the unity of the whole Church, and for all who seek Christ with a sincere heart, that there may be one Flock and one Shepherd.

Lord, hear us.

Father of all goodness, you had pity on your Son, bowed down by suffering. Look with mercy on the poor of this world, our persecuted brethren: visit them with your love and give them your peace. We ask this through Christ our Lord.

Amen.

◆XII◆

JESUS DIES ON THE CROSS

From the sixth hour onwards there was darkness over all the land until the ninth hour; and about the ninth hour Jesus cried out with a loud voice: *Eli, Eli, lamma sabachthani?* ~ that is, 'My God, my God, why have you forsaken me?' Hearing this, some of those who stood by said: "He is calling upon Elijah." And one of them ran to fetch a sponge, which he filled with vinegar and fixed upon a rod, and offered to let him drink; the rest said, "Wait, let us see if Elijah is to come and save him!"

Jesus drank the vinegar, and said, "It is achieved." Then he bowed his head, and yielded up his spirit. (Mt 27:45-49; Jn 19:30)

Meditation

The words uttered on Golgotha bear witness to the depth ~ unique in the history of the world ~ of the evil of the suffering experienced. When Christ says: "My God, my God, why have you abandoned me?", his words are not only an expression of that abandonment which many times found expression in the Old Testament, especially in the Psalms and in particular in that Psalm 22 from which come the words quoted.

Christ perceives in a humanly inexpressible way this suffering which is the rejection by the Father, the estrangement from God. But precisely through this suffering he accomplishes the Redemption, and can say as he breathes his last: "It is achieved."

Apostolic Letter Salvifici Doloris
11th February 1984

Let us pray

We pray for the courageous defenders of justice and truth, that the laying down of their lives may bring forth fruits of peace and love.

Lord, hear us.

Receive, Lord, the souls of all martyrs for the faith without regard for their faults, and bring them all to your eternal banquet in heaven.

Lord, hear us.

Lord, we pray that, as you wished to live our life and die our death even to the experience of abandonment by the Father, give to all our brethren of the Church in need the light and strength of your presence: you who live and reign for ever and ever.

Amen.

✦XIII✦

JESUS IS TAKEN DOWN FROM THE CROSS

And now a man called Joseph came forward, one of the councillors, a good and upright man: he was from Arimathea, and was one of those who waited for the kingdom of God. He it was who approached Pilate and asked to have the body of Jesus. (Lk 23:50-52)

When the body is taken down from the Cross and laid in the Mother's arms, in our mind's eye we glimpse again the moment when Mary accepted the message brought by the angel Gabriel. Once again Jesus is in her arms, as he was in the stable in Bethlehem, during the flight into Egypt, at Nazareth. (*Via Crucis*)

Meditation

"Christ Jesus, though he was in the form of God, did not count equality with God a thing to be grasped, but emptied himself, taking the form of a servant": precisely on Golgotha "he humbled himself and became obedient unto death, even death on a cross" (Phil 2:5-8).

Through faith the Mother shares in the death of her Son, in his redeeming death; and as a sharing in the sacrifice of Christ ~ the new Adam ~ this faith becomes in a certain sense the counterpoise to the dis-obedience and disbelief embodied in the sin of our first parents. Thus teach the Fathers of the Church and especially Saint Irenaeus: "The knot of Eve's disobedience was untied by Mary's obedience; what the virgin Eve bound through her unbelief, Mary loosened by her faith."

Encyclical Letter Redemptoris Mater
25th March 1987

Let us pray

We pray for our Holy Father, that the Holy Spirit may give him consolation and strength, and may preserve him from the snares of the enemy.

Lord, hear us.

We pray for our bishops, priests, and religious, that they may remain faithful to their commitments to the end and, through their example, may be witnesses of your love to the world.

Lord, hear us.

God of mercy, in the Cross of your Son you revealed to us your love and your power. Teach us to discover in the sufferings of all men the image of him who lives and reigns with you and the Holy Spirit for ever and ever.

Amen.

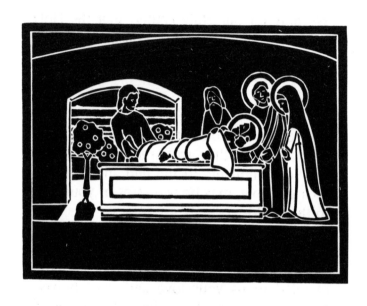

✦XIV✦

JESUS IS LAID IN THE TOMB

With Joseph was Nicodemus, the same who had made his first visit to Jesus by night; he brought with him a mixture of myrrh and aloes, of about a hundred pounds' weight. They took Jesus' body, then, and wrapped it in winding-cloths with the spices: that is how the Jews prepare a body for burial.

In the same quarter where he was crucified there was a garden, with a new tomb in it, one in which no man had ever yet been laid. Here, since the tomb was close at hand, they laid Jesus, rolling a stone against the door of the tomb.

(Jn 19:39-42; Mk 15:46)

Meditation

From the moment when man, because of sin, was banished from the tree of life (Gn 3), the earth became a burial ground. For every human being there is a tomb. In one of the innumerable tombs scattered over this planet of ours, the Son of God, the Man Jesus Christ, conquered death with death. *O mors, ero mors tua* (Lauds of Holy Saturday, 1st Antiphon).

The tree of life from which man was banished because of sin is newly revealed to men in the body of Christ: "If anyone eats this of this bread, he will live for ever. And now, what is this bread which I am to give? It is my flesh, given for the life of the world" (Jn 6:51).

Via Crucis, 14th Station

Let us pray

We pray for those unjustly deprived of the Sacraments, that they may receive the grace and the strength to persevere in union with you.

Lord, hear us.

We pray that we may always find our strength in the Bread of Life and be found worthy, at the end of our lives on earth, to enter into eternal life in heaven.

Lord, hear us.

Lord, we unite ourselves with our fellow-Christians in those places in the world where they are prevented from practising and witnessing to their faith: may our prayer be a supernatural communion with their solitude. We ask this through Christ our Lord.

Amen.

·XV·

CHRIST IS RISEN

At the hour when dawn broke on the first day of the week, Mary Magdalen and the other Mary came near to visit the tomb. And suddenly an angel of the Lord came to the place and rolled away the stone, and sat on it. The angel said openly to the women, "You need not be afraid; I know well that you have come to look for Jesus of Nazareth, the man who was crucified. He is not here: he has risen, as he told you!"

And now it was evening on the same day, the first day of the week; and Jesus came and stood there in their midst: "Peace be upon you," he said. And with that he showed them his hands and his side. So the disciples saw the Lord, and were glad. (Mt 28:1-2, 5-6; Jn 20:19-20)

Meditation

For the women and the apostles, the way opened by the *sign* leads to the meeting with the Risen One: then it is that this still-timid and uncertain perception becomes conviction, and also faith, in him who "is risen indeed".

This is how it is for the women, and particularly for Mary Magdalen... This is how it is for the disciples: when they finally see Jesus in their midst, they are happy with the new certainty that has entered their hearts. Contact with Christ releases the spark that makes faith flare up!

General Audience, 2nd April 1989

Let us pray

We pray for the resurrection of the Church in the many parts of the world where she has been crushed and trampled on by persecution.

Lord, hear us.

We pray that each of us, by our lives and in our words each day, may bear witness to the Risen Christ to all those around us.

Lord, hear us.

We adore your Holy Cross, O Jesus, and we glory in your resurrection. By your death you restored to us our dignity as children of God: give us the grace to share in your redemptive work, spreading the Good News of your Resurrection to every corner of the world, you who live and reign for ever and ever.

Amen.

About **Aid to the Church in Need**

The task of the international Catholic charity **Aid to the Church in Need** is to answer the spiritual and pastoral needs of Catholics everywhere, particularly where the Church is persecuted, oppressed, or in great need.

Founded in 1947 by the Dutch Norbertine priest Werenfried van Straaten, **Aid to the Church in Need** is now an official Church charity directly under the authority of the Pope. With over 7,000 projects in Eastern Europe and throughout the world, it is present today wherever the need is greatest: training seminarians and catechists, building chapels and mission centres, supporting priests, printing Bibles and religious literature, and helping refugees.

You can join the many thousands who support the vital work of this charity with their prayers and their sacrifices. To receive more information, including our bi-monthly newsletter the **Mirror**, please write to our national office.

For more information, contact Aid to the Church in Need

AUSTRALIA
Aid to the Church in Need
c/o North Western Suburbs Mail Centre
3 Powers Road
Seven Hills
2781 NSW
Australia
(0061-2-9679-1929)

CANADA
Aid to the Church in Need
PO Box 1779
St-Laurent
Que. H4L 4Z3
Canada
(001-514-332-6333)

IRELAND
Aid to the Church in Need
151 St Mobhi Road
Glasnevin
Dublin 9
Ireland
(00353-1-83-77-516)

UNITED KINGDOM
Aid to the Church in Need
1 Times Square
Sutton
Surrey SM1 1LF
(0181-642-8668)

USA
Aid to the Church in Need
PO Box 576
2017 Deer Park Avenue
Deer Park
New York 11729-0576
USA
(001-516-242-8321)

Aid to the Church in Need
Meeting the needs of the Church today
in Eastern Europe and throughout the world